The Liberal Zone

It's a strange new world...

by Luke Paulson

The Liberal Zone
It's A Strange New World

Copyright © 2021 by Luke Paulson.

Paperback ISBN: 978-1-63812-161-9
Ebook ISBN: 978-1-63812-162-6

All rights reserved. No part in this book may be produced and transmitted in any form or by any means, electronic, or mechanical, including photocopying, recording, or by any information storage and retrieval system, without permission in writing from the copyright owner.

The views expressed in this work are solely those of the author and do not necessarily reflect the views of the publisher hereby disclaims any responsibility for them.

Published by Pen Culture Solutions   11/10/2021

Pen Culture Solutions
1-888-727-7204 (USA)
1-800-950-458 (Australia)
support@penculturesolutions.com

The Liberal Zone

Table of Contents

1. Changing Him For the Better……………………………………………..01

2. The Child or the Parent……………………………………………09

3. The Masks……………………………………………………15

4. See Her for Who She Is……………………………………………25

5. Untapped Power……………………………………………37

6. What Do You Stand For……………………………………………...43

Chapter 1
Changing Him For the Better

_____

Changing Him For the Better

James and Samuel were walking into the school

"So I saw your mom posted online about how she got a flyer in the mail from the Transition Agency on getting you transitioned."

"Yeah I know, I saw the letter and she got it before I could throw it away. I am not sure that I even want to be transitioned, Sam." James replied.

"Are you kidding? I am super-excited about it, I mean I am going to be transitioned tomorrow! Best of all, I get the day off from school. A double win."

"You don't like the way you are."

"Well, I do, but being transitioned will be much better."

"I do not see why everyone treats it like it's what's best for everyone. It might not be right for me."

"You sound like someone who says the world is flat. Besides, transitioning to a girl is the best part of turning thirteen."

"That sounds like a false comparison to me."

"Whatever, look let's just head off to class and meet up at lunch."

"We all know that gender is an immutable part of who a person is and cannot be changed. Impossible cannot be done even by science. However, impossible is a term that is unheard of in The Liberal Zone."

James knocked on the door of the counselor's office.

"Come in." said the voice inside.

"You wanted to see me, Ms. Branson."

"Yes. Sit down, I just have a few questions about your plans for the future."

"Like what I want to do when I grow up?"

"No, not that. It is just that most kids choose a new name after they transition and you have left yours blank on this registration form. I just wanted to make sure that is what you want."

"I left it blank on purpose ma'am."

"I see. So you want to keep the name James after you transition. I will put that down."

"No Ms. Branson, you don't understand."

"What's that?"

"I do not think that I want to be transitioned at all."

She stared at him for the longest time hardly saying a word. Then she typed something in on her computer before she spoke again.

"This is most unusual. Are you sure about this? Your health and well-being are more important than any second thoughts that you may have."

"I have made my decision and I do not want the procedure."

"There are many options for the procedure, but it is vital to your health and without it, people are more prone to aggressive outbursts and violence. However, I certainly cannot force you to do anything that you do not want to do."

Changing Him For the Better

His mother was ready for him as soon as James walked through the door.

"I remember when I was transitioned. It was such a monumental change in my life and I would never undo it if I could."

"I know mom."

"You don't seem very excited. Are you feeling sick?"

"No, it's not that."

"Your counselor sent me an email earlier today and I am very worried about you. I made an appointment with the doctor to talk about this."

"Isn't it my decision if I want to get transitioned?"

"I care far too much about your mental health to let you turn down one of the most important decisions that you will ever make."

She handed James the tablet as she got up.

"We can talk about some options with the doctor in two days."

James walked home from school the next day without his best friend by his side.

When he came in, his mother told him that someone was there to visit and he should go up to his room.

When he got in there was a girl dressed ready for ballet sitting on his bed.

"Hi, I'm James." He said sticking out his hand.

"Don't you recognize me?"

James stood confused until it dawned on him.

"Sam!"

"Samantha, now." She corrected. "Don't I just look amazing? I cannot wait to go to ballet today. I am finally going to be as graceful as the rest of the advanced class."

James was having trouble processing all of this information.

"Look at the time, I have got to get to practice. I just wanted you to be the first person to see the new me."

As Samantha left, James sat on his bed in deep contemplation.

Sitting around in the doctor's office waiting on her was a bit trying for both of them.

When the doctor came in, she was smiling.

"Ms. Jenner, would you mind giving me a moment alone with James to discuss this?"

"Not at all, doctor." She replied.

Getting up, she turned to James and told him that she would be in the lobby when he was ready.

"Now James. How about you tell me why you don't want to be transitioned."

"I like the way I am. I get good grades, I have never been in trouble and I don't see why I am forced to make the transition if I do not want to."

"Well, it is for your own good. That is why the state mandates the procedure."

"Why?"

"When you study in history class, do you recall any mention of wars?"

"Of course. They were a creation of people for disputes over land or resources in which the people of one country would kill the people of another country to get what they wanted."

"Very good. Now, when is the last recorded incident of a war?"

"I do not know. My teacher says that we don't have much information about them to really make any timeline, especially since there has not been a war in such a long time."

"That is correct. Our country was at war with many other nations for years. Then, psychologists realized a common trait that was found in all wars. They called it 'toxic masculinity'. Surgeons found that the transition was the most effective way to get rid of this trait and save countless lives from the horrors of war."

"Are you saying that the transition stopped the conflicts?"

"Yes, and ever since then, the world has been more peaceful than ever before."

"That's not true. It was all over the news that there was a huge fight at the high school that sent five kids to the hospital."

"Yes, but the report also said that all of those children were transitioned before and there was a minor glitch in their transition surgery that was not reported. The kids were taken in to have it fixed and since then, have been doing just fine."

"Look, I just don't want to change. I like the way I am. I don't want to become someone else."

The doctor looked at her charts for just a moment and then stepped out of the room. She said something to a nurse, but James could not make it out.

The doctor returned with a needle.

"I know, I don't like shots either, but while you are here, your mother wanted you to get this booster."

James rolled up his sleeve and took the shot, but he quickly became woozy and passed out.

His consciousness faded in and out, but he felt as if he was being moved. Eventually, he started to get his senses back and found that he was in an operating room. Before he could even try to fight back, the mask for the anesthesia was lowered and he blacked out again.

Samantha and Caitlyn were waiting in the lobby.

"I just love your dress ma'am."

"Why thank you, dear."

"Samantha, Ms. Jenner, you are both just in time."

"Is it over? I have been so worried about him."

"Well, you don't need to worry anymore."

"It is so upsetting not being able to comfort James in this time."

"As I am sure you know, occasionally a young man has trouble adjusting to the idea of the transition, but after some simple reasoning, they always see the light."

"So, do we need to schedule an appointment for his transition?"

"Not at all, we had a spot open up at the last minute. And she prefers to be called Luna now."

Luna runs out excited about the way that she looks.

"Mother! Mother Samantha, look at me what do you think?"

Samantha went back to hug her bestie.

"We both look amazing! Do you think that you can get me a spot to do ballet with you?"

"I don't see why not. We are going to have so much fun together."

"Come on girls, let's go to the mall. Luna is going to need a whole new wardrobe."

The three walk out.

"Humanity has questioned the nature of science and how it affects us since the beginning of time. However, what happens when someone is forced to change who they are with science? Such a strange and unusual world might not happen tomorrow, but it happens now in The Liberal Zone."

Chapter 2
The Child or The Parent

The Child or the Parent

Billy walked in through the front door and found his dad sitting in his easy chair thinking very deeply.

"Hi, dad!"

"Hello, son. Sit down, we need to talk."

"Things are tough lately and a lot of jobs are getting cut at the plant and I could be next. We really have to tighten our belts."

"I understand dad. Just let me know if there is anything that I can do."

"Nothing right now, but go up there and study, we need you to keep that scholarship."

"There are few things more damaging to the relationship between a father and his son than financial instability. Money can cause a rift in even the most moral of individuals. Joseph Jones and his son Billy will soon find out how deep this rift can be, in The Liberal Zone."

The next day at school, the plant closing was all his friends could talk about.

"That plant must employ nearly half the town in one way or another."

"If they really are talking about letting people go, everyone in this town is going to be in serious trouble."

"Billy, didn't you say that Pastor Jeff offered assistance to your dad so that you could stay here."

The Child or the Parent

"Yeah. However, my dad is far too prideful to take any handouts like that. The only reason he is letting me keep this scholarship is that we don't have any other option. He does not want me to help because that would take time away from my studies."

"Dude, you make perfect scores on every test! Mrs. Martin actually thought you were cheating because you did so well."

"I know, but my dad does not want to risk it. I even tried making some extra money, but it did not work out at all."

"What happened?"

"Well first I tried collecting cans for recycling to make a little extra, but the governor enacted an edict making it illegal because a gang was breaking into dumps to get cans. Then I tried opening a lemonade stand, with your mom's help, as you recall. The police actually showed up and told me that I did not have a permit to sell. Then I thought at least I can mow lawns; that is something that I know how to do. Turns out my gas-powered mower is not up to environmental standards. My dad was furious because they would not have found out if I had not gone looking for work. Now, he has to buy a new mower on top of all of this."

"Well, maybe we can get our parents to help."

"Yeah, I am sure that they would be more than willing."

"Sorry guys, but my dad has told me explicitly and without hesitation that I am not to do that at all. He means well and I am sure that he knows what he is doing."

The next day, Billy stopped by the post office to get the mail. He noticed a flyer for the Children's Agency. A lot of these flyers were going around since the plant was closing.

The Child or the Parent

Their advertisements were always on television. Not that Billy ever got a chance to watch any television, his father had to sell their TV to have money for food.

When he brought the flyer home his father's eyes had a gleam unlike what he had ever seen before.

After dinner, his father called the Children's Agency and although he could not make out much of the conversation, it seemed to be good news.

As Billy got ready for school, he went into his father's room.

"Is the Children's Agency going to be able to help us?" Billy asked.

"They are. However, with the plant closing, it may be a few days before they can help us."

When Billy came home the next day, his dad told him to put the mail on the table and to go straight to his room to work on homework. He would call him down when dinner was ready.

Billy noticed that his father was slightly more hopeful than he had ever been it was almost as if his father had some plan about what to do to fix their otherwise hopeless mess.

After a little while, he heard the doorbell ring and Mr. Jones told him to get the door.

Billy came out of his room and went to answer the door as he was told.

Two intimidating men were standing at the door and showed him a badge.

"Young man, are you William Ted Jones?" one of the two men gruffly asked.

"I am" Billy answered with considerable fear in his voice.

The Child or the Parent

"My name is Agent Ortez and this is my associate Agent Smith. Is your father home?" Asked Agent Ortez.

"He is," Billy answered.

"Good, please tell him that we are here." Agent Smith demanded.

"Okay," Billy said as he began to close the door.

"No," said Agent Ortez as he put his hand in the way. "Leave the door open son."

Now Billy was more frightened than he was before as he went into the kitchen, he could barely put the words together.

"Dad, there are two men that are here and want to talk to you."

"That is strange, I was not expecting them tonight."

"Who are they, dad?"

"Don't worry about that son, let's just go and talk to them."

They walked up to the door and although Billy tried to hide behind his father, this was to no avail. His father ensured that his son was front and center.

"Gentlemen, I did not expect to see you here so soon. Are you with the Agency?"

"We are." Said Agent Smith.

"The Agency likes us to be very prompt in matters such as this." Agent Ortez continued.

"I assume you are Joseph Ted Jones. We have already been introduced to your son. Is now a good time?" Agent Smith continued.

The Child or the Parent

"Oh, now is a perfect time. I am so glad that you people are around to help me with my problem."

With that, he pushed his son forward and Agent Smith grabbed the small boy's arm.

"What's going on? Daddy, what is happening?" Billy wailed.

"We will send you the pertinent paperwork first thing in the morning." Agent Ortez said as his partner dragged the small child kicking down the block.

Agent Smith had produced a sock to place in Billy's mouth to prevent him from screaming too much while his partner was talking to Joseph.

Billy was placed in the back of their car as Joseph calmly closed the door and began to eat supper beside Billy's empty place setting.

"It is said that the love of money is the root of all evil. However, can this same love truly convince a father to surrender that which should be protected most of all? A question that is shelved within the deepest confines of The Liberal Zone."

Chapter 3
The Masks

The Masks

Grace was just sobbing right outside the courtroom while her friend tried to comfort her.

"Grace, we tried to warn you that this would happen. You just do not go against the grain. We are a nation of laws. There are rules that you have to follow and being a rebel just because you don't like what the doctors say does not help anyone."

"An ounce of prevention is worth a pound of cure, but can prevention go too far? Now disgraced Dr. Grace Wilson has to maintain some semblance of her former life while trapped within The Liberal Zone."

ONE YEAR AGO

"Let's talk about how to determine the proper medication and dosage. It is vitally important to know your patient before prescribing them their medication. Even the smallest details can severely affect the efficacy of any drug that you may need to prescribe. Gender is a factor as many drugs will affect tissue unique to men and women and can cause dangerous and even life-threatening side effects. This is especially dangerous with anything that has hormones or steroids. Age is an important factor as well. How many of you have seen a warning on a bottle of children's medicine warning against driving or operating machinery while taking it? Now we know that children do not normally drive or operate machinery, so can anyone tell me why there would be this notice?"

Raising his hand, "Because of the child's size and metabolism, he cannot take as much of the drug that an adult should. Therefore if an adult will often convert the child's dosage to an adult dosage to achieve the desired effect."

"That is correct."

The Masks

"Age is a factor as well as height and body weight. Oftentimes, these medications will list an age range for dosage, but these are not set in stone. Some children mature faster than others and some have more efficient metabolisms than others."

"Yes, you have a question."

"Dr. Wilson, how can you determine a lot of this without being able to see the person?"

"That is an excellent question, many times you will have to ask the patient to lift their mask and look from afar or look at their ID card. Other times, if you know the patient, you can know a lot more about the patient than you would learn from asking questions off of a checklist."

"Finally remember that all drugs interact with each other. For example, antipsychotic drugs can be rendered less effective with the use of alcohol. This applies not just to beer and wine, but since there is a small amount of alcohol in most cold medicines, it can be a factor. If rendered less effective, the hallucinations can and very well may return."

Just then, the dean walked into the classroom with some paperwork in his hands.

"Class, I think we are going to end right there for today. Next class, we will continue to look at how to measure prescription drug use."

As the class files out, the dean approaches the podium.

"Justin, what can I do for you today?"

"I found this video online about the virus and I wanted to get your opinion on it."

"Of course, I will always be happy to give my opinion."

He pulls out his phone and has a video of Dr. Grace giving a lecture over a green screen.

The Masks

"Viruses are extremelty fragile things and I explained in last week's video. There are lots of things that can kill a virus such as soap and water, heat, certain medications, and ultraviolet light. Doctors sterilize their equipment using ultraviolet light because it is more efficient than using soap and water. Imagine if you will, a very low level ultraviolet light that was in the wind pipe just above the lungs. It could kill a large portion of this or any other virus. This technology is very easily…"

The Dean cut off the feed and put his phone back in his pocket.

"I am confused, what do you need my opinion on if that was my personal YouTube channel."

"It is getting a lot of attention and is being shared across social media."

"That is great, with more discussion and debate, we can work towards putting this virus down and opening up medical research to things like cancer and Alzheimer's."

"Not really, Grace. You are propping up a medical treatment that has been rejected by the National Science Board and the International Medical Alliance."

"If you watch the rest of the video, I did mention that, but I also mentioned several things that both agencies have said that were proven to be wrong later with no consequences whatsoever."

"Grace, it is not our place to question what the experts say, especially if they are above our pay grade. Furthermore, the board is not at all pleased as since you are employed by the university, this reflects badly on us and it makes it seem as if the university is endorsing this pseudo-science."

The Masks

The dean unfolded the sheet of paper that he was carrying.

"I am going to ask you to make a retraction video and sign this paper saying that you will no longer post anything to your personal blog without first sending it by my office for approval."

"Sir, I cannot do that. I provided medical expertise and backed it up with my own clinical trials."

"Very well, effective immediately, you are suspended pending an official investigation. However, I do not expect things to go very well with the board. The president is already considering your termination as it is."

"But, I…"

"I am sorry Grace, you may as well start cleaning out your office."

SIX MONTHS AGO

Grace put away the IVs from dinner and then sat down in her chair. She had spent the day applying to every medical facility and agency in the city. Naturally, she was exaughsted.

No one would hire someone who had been fired so disgracefully.

There were a few people who still supported her. She still made some videos in her spare time on her backup channel.

The university had taken down her previous channel since more than half of her videos were recorded with the university logo in the background and they could no longer be associated with her in any way.

Her daughter Evelyn was getting ready for her first day of kindergarten tomorrow.

The Masks

There was only one major thing that she was worried about now. Eve had a breathing problem and wearing her mask frequently brought on hypertension and anxiety.

Grace had put special inserts into Eve's mask to make it easier for her to breathe, but those inserts were not allowed in school.

"Eve, could you come down here sweetie?"

Running downstairs, Eve came up to her mom, fidgeting with her mask as always.

"Honey, you have to stop fidgeting, your teacher is not going to like that."

"But mommy, it is so hard to breathe, why did you have to take out my inserts."

"The school does not allow that, because then you could spread the virus to someone else."

Eve suddenly stopped fidgeting.

"You are getting to be a big girl now, you have to learn to wear your mask like everybody else."

The next day at the temp agency, Grace already had a call come in as soon as she sat down at her desk.

"This is Grace Wilson. How may I help you?"

"This is Nurse Simmons. We need you to come down to the school right away."

"Why, is something wrong?"

"It is your daughter, Grace. She passed out not too long ago due to the stress of her new environment and she might need you here."

The Masks

"Of course, I will be there right away!"

When she arrived, Evelyn was breathing deeply trying to regain her composure in between sobs.

"What happened, sweetie?"

"I don't know, I put some inserts that I made out of cardboard into my mask and my teacher made me take them out."

"Honey, I warned you about that."

"I know Mommy. After a while, it got really hard to breathe and the next thing I knew, I was here."

"I will see what I can do about allowing some inserts to your mask."

ONE MONTH AGO

"Your honor, I must ask that you reconsider this order, Eve has an anxiety problem and has trouble breathing. She is not an isolated incident. Just last week there was a school in Fortran City that forcibly put another strap on a child's mask and he passed out from hypoxia. There are dozens of children that pass out not just due to hypoxia, but also from anxiety and stress as a direct result of masks.

"What would you propose Ms. Wilson? I would like to remind you that your description of these events does not match what the experts have been telling us over the years."

"I am asking the court to allow inserts into my child and others that are affected this way to make it easier to breathe."

The Masks

"I am sorry ma'am, but if we do this it would open the floodgates. There is already significant pushback from people like you to not wear masks at all. I am afraid that if I authorized this exception, it would only cause an incentive for more anti-scientific falsehoods to creep in and people would stop wearing masks preventing all that we have accomplished in stopping the spread of this virus."

"But I…"

"Ms. Wilson, this court has other matters to deal with and will not argue any further. Please exit the courtroom at once. Next case!"

PRESENT DAY

"Ms. Wilson, I understand that you have been homeschooling your daughter these past few weeks is this correct?"

"Yes, your honor, it has been very difficult, but we are making it work."

"As I understand it, you have been placing these inserts into your child's mask despite being ordered by this court not to do so."

"Your honor, when we go to the grocery store or to the bank, she does not wear the inserts. only when we are at home and she is wearing her mask the whole time."

"Since you are disgraced from the medical community, allow me to read from the official guidelines from the Education Department and hopefully you can understand. This is from Chapter 2 Paragraph 3 Section A

"Children will have the required vaccinations each year as required by paragraph 4 of this document when they begin school, this is not just for those interacting with other students, but for those who will be learning at home as well. Since these students will play outside as well and will interact with others, these vaccinations are therefore required by all students."

"Do you have any questions about that document? It is available with the paperwork that you received at the start of the school year as well as when you applied to homeschool your daughter. Did you receive this paperwork?"

"Yes your honor, I did indeed receive this paperwork and I have documented evidence that all of the vaccines have been accounted for before the first day of school."

"Yet, you continue to let her wear these inserts in her mask."

"Yes, there is no requirement against the inserts in the law that you just read."

"That may be so, but this virus is even more dangerous than anything that children are vaccinated against. Yet somehow, you think these inserts are safe."

"I do your honor. In addition to homeschooling, and my remote temp job, I have been doing significant research on this virus and…"

"Ms. Wilson, as has been stated before, you have no authority in this department and it seems that you value pseudo-science over empirical data. I am hereby granting a motion to the state to consider that your daughter be removed from your care since you are clearly incapable of caring for a child."

"But you can't do that!"

"I can and I just did."

"Please I beg…"

The Masks

"Quiet, leave this courtroom immediately or the bailiff will escort you out."

Grace was just sobbing right outside the courtroom while her friend tried to comfort her.

"Grace, we tried to warn you that this would happen. You just do not go against the grain. We are a nation of laws. There are rules that you have to follow and being a rebel just because you don't like what the doctors say does not help anyone."

Eventually, she did leave the courtroom but insisted on doing so alone.

"It is important to stand up for what you believe in. However, sometimes the cost can be higher than you anticipated. Everyone must pay the price, especially in The Liberal Zone."

Chapter 4
See Her For Who She Is

See Her For Who She Is

Jennifer awkwardly stood at the front of the class as the teacher introduced her as a new student.

"Class, I want you all to give a warm welcome to our newest student, Jennifer Morrison."

"Thank you, Ms. Simmons."

"Please take a seat over there and we will get started."

Jennifer tried to sit down in one of the two empty desks, but another girl indicated that she sit at the other.

"That is Jay's desk, she is running late today."

Ms. Simmons began her lecture as most of the class zoned out.

As the lecture went on, a boy wearing the girl's uniform tried to slip in unnoticed. Without turning around…

"Jay, it is nice of you to join us. I hope you enjoyed your extra time today because you will be serving detention after school for being tardy."

Jay begrudgingly sat down next to Jennifer.

"Hi Jay, I'm Jennifer."

"Yeah, I heard we had a new girl today."

"So, did you lose a bet or something?"

"Why do you think that I lost a bet?"

"Well, you are a boy that is wearing the school uniform for girls, so…"

See Her For Who She Is

"I Am A Girl!"

"Jay! I will not tolerate you shouting in my classroom."

"But Ms. Simmons!"

"Not one more, young lady or you will have detention for the rest of the week."

"Ms. Simmons, Jennifer said that Jay was a boy."

"Oh. Well, Jennifer, I am not sure what they taught you at your old school, but here we treat people with respect. Now apologize to Jay."

"Yes, Ms. Simmons. I'm sorry Jay."

"It's alright, I should not have gotten so upset."

"Now that, that is over, let's continue with today's lesson."

> **"When a group is running towards a cliff, the only one who stops at the edge is thought a fool. Imagine being that one voice and still unable to stop those who jump over the cliff right into The Liberal Zone."**

"Come on girls it should not take you this long to get ready for gym!"

The class slowly filed out into the gymnasium.

Blowing her whistle, "Alright girls. Pair up and I want you to do sit-ups and switch when I blow my whistle again."

Jennifer held Elaine's legs while she did sit-ups.

"So tell me, why is Jay wearing a girl's uniform?"

"Are you still on that? Girls wear the girl's uniforms and boys wear the boy's uniforms, there is nothing wrong with that."

"She looks like a boy in a dress."

"Well, it does not matter what she looks like, the fact remains that she is a girl."

"Something does not feel right."

"Is it because she was checking you out in the locker room?"

"Wait! What?"

"Yeah, Jay must have found something about you that she likes. I mean, I guess I don't see it since I am not into other girls…"

"That is so invasive."

"Look, she has checked most of us out every day, it is just something that you have to deal with when a girl likes other girls."

"Look, I…"

The coach blew her whistle and the two switched.

"You were saying…"

"Something does not feel right."

"Well, your feelings do not make facts and quite frankly I do not want to talk about it anymore because you are sounding incredibly insensitive."

"I really think the way that I feel about someone else checking me out is of some importance."

"Listen here, new girl…"

The coach blew her whistle.

"Alright girls, give me 20 laps around the gym. Anyone who does not complete the circuit or tries to take a shortcut will have detention for a week!"

With that, she blew her whistle and the girls started jogging.

"Either way, I think you should look into Ethan. He sits right behind you and he could not take his eyes off of you all day."

"Wait really? Is he cute?"

"He is the fifth grade's most eligible bachelor. We're going to lunch right after this, I'll introduce you."

In the cafeteria, the girls got their trays and Jennifer was about to reach for the ketchup dispenser for her fries, but Elaine stopped her.

"I would not use that one, it tends to squirt out all over the place. And trust me, you do not want to get a ketchup stain on a white shirt."

"Thanks. I guess my fries will taste okay without ketchup."

"He usually sits over here."

"Elaine, it is so nice to see you."

"Hi Ethan, I am sure that you remember Jennifer from class."

"Yeah, of course, I do, granted I did not see much, but the back of her head."

"Well, now you can... Oh, darn it, I forgot that I was supposed to be having lunch with Susan and Nicole today! I'll catch you guys later."

"Something tells me that she wanted to leave us alone."

"Yeah, but I don't mind. I usually sit by myself, but it is nice to have some company, especially…"

Jennifer was in the bathroom washing her hands when Jay came in.

Jennifer tried to walk out, but Jay would not let her leave.

"I could not help but notice you in gym class today and I heard that you were talking about me to Elaine. I cannot help, but feel as if we have some sort of connection."

Jay was slowly getting closer, but Jennifer was too scared to do anything.

"I mean, I like you and you obviously like me, why don't we make it official."

"What do you mean?"

"I mean that I want to plant one on you right now."

Before Jennifer could even react, she was against the wall and locked in Jay's embrace.

As some of the girls walked in and saw the spectacle, they ran out and it was not long before the entire school knew about the event.

As Jay leaned back out, she had the biggest smile on her face.

"That was amazing, maybe next time, I can sneak in some lip gloss and we can have fun."

At lunch the next day, Jennifer went to go and sit with Ethan. He let her sit down, but would not say anything for several minutes.

"I thought we had something special, Jennifer! I like you a lot."

"I like you a lot too."

"Then what were you doing kissing Jay in the girls' room? The whole school knows about it."

"She kissed me."

"I guess, you did not resist that much."

"She is strong and sick."

"Well if she is sick, it should not be that hard."

"I mean in her head."

"Now you are just insulting her for no reason. If you don't mind, I would rather eat my lunch in peace. I don't have time for someone who cheats on me on day one."

With tears in her eyes, Jennifer found another place to sit.

Jennifer heard someone sit down beside her. She turned to look and it was Jay.

"Mind if I sit here?"

"I guess I can't stop you, Jay. You are the reason that I am in this mess in the first place."

"Look, maybe I was forceful, but there is nothing wrong with a make-out session between two girls."

"Listen, you are a boy. And I for one…"

"I guess you are the only one who thinks that."

With that Jay walked off, for some reason, Jennifer could not help but feel the slightest bit of pity for her.

When Jennifer got back to class, Ms. Simmons gave her a note to go to the principal's office.

"How am I going to explain this to my parents?" she muttered under her breath.

When she got to the office, Jay and another adult were there as well.

"Hello, Jennifer. I understand that you know Jay and this is Mrs. Worth, the school counselor."

"What is this all about?"

"Jay says that in the short time that you have been here, you have never let up on how you seem to think that she is a boy in a skirt. I cannot imagine why you would think something so bizarre, but here we are. Do you have anything to say for yourself?"

"Well, Jay is a boy."

"Jennifer, you cannot just let your feelings explain this, Jay is a girl," said Mrs. Worth.

"She is right young lady and such bigotry has no place on this campus. I am sending you home for the rest of the day and if you engage in any more bigotry towards Jay, I will consider having you suspended."

Jennifer slowly walked out of the office and to the front door.

See Her For Who She Is

That night, Jennifer was very quiet at dinner, she knew that her parents knew about all of this, but refused to say anything herself.

"So," her father began. "Do you want to tell us why you got sent home today?"

"There was a boy that was wearing a girl's uniform and…"

"Enough young lady. I do not care what you think about Jay. Your principal explained the entire situation. Facts are facts and do not care about your opinion."

"Your father is right dear. You need to follow the facts and treat Jay for the person that she is." Her mother said.

The next day, Jennifer was practically walking on eggshells, not wanting to say anything about Jay, lest she get suspended.

As she was walking down the hallway, she found a discarded folder.

Instead of bringing it straight to the lost and found, her curiosity got the best of her and she decided to take a look inside.

To say that she was shocked was an understatement. She flipped through the pages in the folder, and all of them were just as shocking.

She went straight to the office. The secretary instantly tried to stop her, but Jennifer was on a mission.

"Principal Wilson, I have to speak with you!"

Just then the secretary had caught up…

"Come on and get back to class young lady. I am so sorry about this sir."

"It is alright Jane. Clearly, there is something important going on."

The secretary left and the two were alone.

"So, Jennifer, tell me what this is all about."

"I found this folder in the hallway and its contents are disturbing to say the least."

Principal Wilson took one glance and shut the folder immediately.

"I wish you had warned me as to what I was going to see," he stuttered.

"I am sorry sir, I did not know what else to do."

"Jane, would you call Mrs. Worth in here? It is a bit urgent."

"While we are waiting, do you know whose folder this is?"

"No sir, I do not."

With a small knock on the door frame, Mrs. Worth came in.

"Thank you for coming so quickly, please close the door. Jennifer here has brought this folder to my attention and I was about to ask her how she came about it."

"May I see the folder, Mr. Wilson?"

"Sure thing, but I have to warn you that the contents are rather shocking."

Mrs. Worth looked at the contents of the folder.

"These are pictures from inside the girl's locker room and from the bathroom."

"Yes, we need to look for the cameras, wherever they are, and take them down."

"That may be harder to do than you think sir, from what I can tell, these photos look like they were taken in person."

"Jennifer, I know that you have only been here a few days, but have you seen anything unusual that might help?"

"Well, is there any girl that does not appear in any of the photos? Whoever that is might be the one taking the photos."

"That is true, and I will look into this. Such a grievous invasion of privacy cannot and must not be tolerated. Do you need to go and sit in my office or are you okay to go back to class?"

"Thank you, Mrs. Worth, but I think that I will be fine. I think I will head straight to class."

"Now, Jennifer before you go, I do not want you to mention this to anyone. We have to catch this person and she cannot know that we are on to her."

"I understand sir."

The rest of the day was increasingly awkward especially when it came to gym. Jennifer knew that there was someone there taking photos of the girls and that only made it harder.

Mr. Wilson flagged her down in the hallway and invited her into his office.

"Jennifer, while I am happy that you brought that folder to my attention, our investigation has found that no member of the faculty, student body, or outside force will be held responsible. Furthermore, you are to never mention this incident to anyone ever again."

"But then who took the pictures?" Jennifer inquired.

"Just leave it be and go to class."

Jennifer walked out and went to class. Over the next few days, even more of the folders were found all over the school and every time that Jennifer brought it to a teacher, they just told her to forget about it.

Eventually, Jennifer began comparing the photos and found what she suspected all along, the only person who was never in a photo was Jay.

"The sole voice of reason in a room is overlooked in favor of majority opinion. Unable to warn another about a lie that they have trapped themselves is a terrifying dilemma, in or out of The Liberal Zone."

Chapter 5
Untapped Power

Untapped Power

John walked out of his house with a bucket ready to scrub the day's graffiti off of his home. Today's included the usual statements:

"I BURN THE RAINFORESTS"

And…

"HOW MUCH DO YOU DUMP IN RIVERS".

While this was annoying and painstaking to clean up, the police refused to do anything as long as there was no threat being made. Every other home had a roof full of solar panels to eat up every bit of sunshine that came through.

It was a particularly hot day and so John brought some lemonade out with him as he scrubbed the walls. He was listening to the news as he scrubbed and turned it on just as the weather report came on.

"Good morning, everyone and today is going to be a day to stay in with the A/C on all day. This record-breaking heatwave has no end in sight and it is going to be sunny all day long with hardly a cloud in the sky. Expect a high of 115°. Multiple house fires across the city have been submitted and the burn ban is still in place. There are of course people pointing out that the fires have started in homes and businesses that have rooftop solar panels, but that is just a coincidence. This large increase in fires is a direct result of global warming and man-made climate change. These comments are just designed to attack people who are taking strong steps to reverse the damage to Mother Earth."

"I wish I had gotten started on this earlier, but I should be done before long."

Untapped Power

"Submitted for your perusal, one Mr. John Henry continues to stay connected to the coal-powered electrical grid. What is the cost of this energy? Therein lies our tale, deep within The Liberal Zone."

John sat in his office typing at his computer. It was time-consuming work, but it was good honest work.

As he typed, he suddenly heard rain falling on the window.

Turning off the recording that he was transcribing he turned to look out the window. He turned on the news.

"Impossible!"

"We now go to Anthony Rora with the weather."

"Thank you, as I am sure all of you can tell, we had a sudden and I do mean a sudden freak rainstorm. Satellite data shows that this storm has blanketed half of the state. As you can see from these pictures, the clouds materialized out of thin air. Rest assured, that I am sharing data with my colleagues across the state and with the National Weather Service to understand what brought this on. There does not seem to be any dangerous pollutants in the water, so it should be safe for gardens. However, we do not know how much of the rain will seep into the soil and so the burn ban has not been lifted as of the present."

After a few hours, the rain finally stopped coming down, but the clouds were not clearing up, John turned the news back on.

"We now take you to Anthony Rora for an update."

"Thank you, it seems the rain has universally stopped, but the unique cloud formation has yet to dissipate. I have learned from one of my colleagues that although there are no dangerous substances in the cloud formation, they seem to be bound together by some as of yet unknown force. Because of this, we fear that they will not break up any time soon. Please do not panic as I am sure that our most brilliant minds can find a solution to the problem."

As the days went on, more and more people were without power as their homes and businesses could no longer keep their lights on, but John kept his lights on.

He needed the time to clean up the graffiti on the side of his house that had only increased. Phrases such as:

"COAL BROKE THE SKY"

And…

"I CAUSED THE BLACKOUT"

Were incredibly common.

"If these clouds do not clear up soon, I may have more to worry about than just cleaning up paint," John mused.

Anthony Rora was at a loss for words to explain what happened.

"Normally, large cloud formations like this indicate high pressure, that creates the wind, but so far the skies are incredibly calm and I do not know what to make of it. I do know that everywhere these clouds are, the wind is almost non-existent. I am sure that you have heard the reports of similar phenomena all over the world and we can independently verify that they are true. They seem to center over parts of the world where large mining operations are taking place.

It seems that the Earth is acting negatively to all of mankind's mining operations and striking back."

Over the next few days, John was one of the only people in town that had any electricity at all. That night, he awoke to shouts outside of his bedroom window.

"Get out here Henry!"

"Yeah get out of your carbon-pumping house!"

"People like you destroyed the sky and are ruining our lives."

"I did not do anything to the skies, I am in dire straits just like you! I had to put on a sweater to go to bed."

"Why not just burn down the rainforest to keep warm!"

"Why would I burn down the rainforest? That makes no sense!"

All the while, John was dialing 911 trying to get the police, but the operator would not pick up.

"Stop pumping coal into the air or we will drag you out and tear this house down!"

"Is that a threat?!"

"No, it is a promise."

Just then, someone threw something at the window where John was looking out and he instinctively closed the window just in time. Although he was unhurt, there was a universal cry from the mob downstairs.

"He retreated into his bunker; we have to get him out now!"

With that, the front door did not last long and John was dragged out of his house.

"It seems that you will never stop polluting and destroying our home and so if we burn down your house, maybe you will learn your lesson."

"That will just put more carbon into the atmosphere."

"That does not matter, we have to do whatever it takes to stop the use of coal." One of the men said as he threw the first torch into John's house.

"No!" he screamed as the crowd held him back.

"If we just get rid of the polluters, we can finally get the sun back."

John was forced to watch his home burn to the ground while the mob cheered.

"Over the next few days the people of the town would learn that it was not just any mining operation that caused the formation, but a reaction from the mines to obtain lithium and cobalt for batteries. Coal mines and oil rigs were devoid of this other-worldly formation. However, this revelation was found far too late for one innocent John Henry, a victim of The Liberal Zone."

Chapter 6
What Do You Stand For?

What Do You Stand For?

The statue of the Civil War soldier dominated the sleepy little town of Jefferson Harbor, Louisiana. A masked mob approached the statue with ropes ready to tear down the painful monument that represented that divisive Civil War a century and a half ago.

Armed men stood in front of the statue looking to defend it.

Both sides stood by quietly each watching the other closely to see who would make the first move.

Nathan decided to run in and take his chances and his compatriots came with him. It was a truly horrible sight to see, but in the chaos, Nathan was hit over the head with the blunt end of a rifle.

"Come on son, get up." came a soothing voice.

The room was dark lit only by a single oil lamp in the corner. When Nathan finally came to, he saw a kindly old woman by his bedside.

"I am so glad to see that you are up. You gave us quite the fright, my kids found you outside in the woods and my husband Eli brought you here to get better."

"Who… Who are you? Where am I?"

"My name is Rhetha Washington and you are in the quaint little town of Jefferson Harbor, Louisiana."

"History is a difficult subject for most people since we cannot observe it happening in real-time. However, Nathan Bedson is about to get an up-close and personal view of history, courtesy of The Liberal Zone."

What Do You Stand For?

"Are you part of some historical re-enactment or something?"

"Why boy, whatever are you talking about?" Rhetha asked.

Nathan could hardly put into words exactly what he was feeling. He started to get up.

"Easy there, young man." Rhetha held him back. "You get too excited, you're liable to hurt yourself."

She helped him to his feet and thanked her for her hospitality.

"What a strange woman," he thought as he walked out the door.

As he stepped out, the world suddenly looked like one of his history textbooks about the 1800s. While he was still staring off into space, he heard a man's voice.

"Well, look who woke up from his nap."

Nathan turned to see the voice and found a man getting ready to chop some wood on the stump of a tree.

"Would a strapping young lad like yourself mind giving me a hand? I have to finish chopping the wood so that the missus can cook dinner."

"I have never chopped wood before. I do not think that I know how." Nathan explained.

"How do you not know how to chop wood? Are you an escaped slave or something?"

"I am nobody's slave, I never have been and I never will be!"

"Well, there is no need to get defensive about it. Most folks around here are freed and are trying to make our lives unloading freight from the docks."

What Do You Stand For?

Nathan could not figure out what was going on. While he was still pondering this, he heard a church bell ring in the distance.

"It's a little late for services, don't you think?"

Before he even finished, Eli had run past him toward the bell.

"Get that wood inside. Stay with the missus and kids, I will be back as soon as I can."

It took him more than a few trips to get all of the wood into the house. By the time he was done, with one trip, Rhetha was waiting on some more to put on the stove and by the fireplace.

Nathan sat down at the table with the kids and enjoyed the supper that was so graciously prepared for him.

The children were in bed by the time that Eli got home. He sat down at the table, the food was cold, but he did not seem to mind. He was focused on something very pressing.

It was a long time before he opened up about it.

"Union soldiers burned down the plantation just north of here." Eli finally explained.

"My goodness!" Rhetha gasped. "Why would they do something like that?"

"It was a spot where major military decisions were being made for the Confederacy."

While Nathan wanted to say something about it, he held his tongue, he reasoned that they must have done it to free the enslaved people there.

"That is not the worst part of all of it." Eli continued. "They would not let anyone leave the plantation as it burned to the ground, the soldiers shot any slave trying to escape thinking that they might be escaping with military secrets."

What Do You Stand For?

"That can't be true!" Nathan shouted.

"Quiet boy!" Rhetha scolded.

"Only a handful of people got out and that is what the meeting at the church was about." Eli went on.

"Do you think that they could be heading this way?" Rhetha asked.

"I would not doubt it, this is one of the most important port cities before New Orleans. If those soldiers get here, it will mean a major blow to the war effort."

"Wait, I thought the Union was trying to free the slaves. What is going on?" Nathan asked.

"Whoever told you that, sold you a load of nonsense. Yes, that is what they were told to do, but they will burn down a town to stop our soldiers and will kill any man Colored or White."

"What are we going to do? This is where we were raised and our parents before us." Rhetha worriedly asked.

"We are putting together a militia. If they come here, we are going to do whatever we can to hold them off." Eli explained.

"What chance do we possibly have against an army?" Nathan asked.

"Not much, but we have to try. Do you know how to shoot boy?"

Nathan did not believe in guns, but could not say why to Eli.

"No, my dad never did have a chance to show me."

What Do You Stand For?

"Well, you are old enough to learn. We need all the help we can get. Will you help protect this town?"

"After what you just told me, I will gladly defend this town from any and all who want to harm it."

"We had best get to bed, training starts first thing in the morning."

Nathan and Eli got up at the crack of dawn. The camp was just outside the town.

Nathan and the other young men that had never learned to shoot yet were in charge of making sure that everyone had the supplies that they needed.

"Go into the woods boy and get as much wood as you can carry. Take a few of the others with you." An older soldier commanded Nathan.

Nathan took them and began gathering wood. The other boys were getting even more than they could carry and had to leave some of what they had gathered behind.

While they were getting ready to go back, Nathan heard some very distinctive chatter. It was not from the direction of the camp. Nathan sent the other boys back and he went to investigate the noise. His worst fears were realized when he saw Union troops setting up camp just outside of the woods.

"Our scouts have reported that there is a militia on the north side of town." Said, one officer.

"If that is where they are making their stand, we will just go around them." Said another.

"The town will be destroyed if they go around." He thought to himself. "I have to warn everyone."

What Do You Stand For?

As he backed away, he stepped on a fallen branch. The distinctive crunch alerted the soldiers to his presence.

"It's a spy, shoot him!"

A volley of bullets came in his direction. He came to the camp and quickly drew a crowd.

"The Union forces are on the other side of the forest and they are planning to go around our forces to attack the town from the south!"

"Sergeant Eli, take a contingent down there and use skirmishes to pick them off."

"Yes sir!"

"The rest of you, are with me, we are going to defend the side of the town where they are coming through."

Nathan tried to stand up, but could not.

One of the nurses helped him get to the field hospital, he had only just realized that he had been hit by one of their bullets.

It seemed like hours before the main forces returned, but they returned victorious against the enemy forces.

Eli likewise returned only having lost a handful of men.

The general came to Nathan's bedside and taking off his hat…

"What you did saved this entire town and we will not easily forget it."

He saluted Nathan who saluted back to him as he slowly bled out.

What Do You Stand For?

On the other side of the tent was a soldier drawing on a large sheet of paper.

"What you got there private?" Eli asked.

The soldier turned the paper around.

"It is a picture of that brave soldier who helped protect us all."

"Do you know how to sculpt?" Eli asked.

"I do indeed."

The next week had a huge unveiling ceremony overseen by Eli and after a bit of fanfare, Eli pulled the cloth off of the statue.

A statue was unveiled of Nathan with the simple plaque:

"PRIVATE NATHAN BEDSON, WHOSE QUICK ACTION LED TO STOPPING UNION FORCES FROM DESTROYING THE TOWN OF JEFFERSON HARBOR."

The statue stood for years until it was eventually torn down by rioters 150 years later.

"What difference does a handful of generations make in how we perceive the world? Just like Nathan Bedson, you might find out that you oppose the very principles that your forefathers fought to defend. A lesson that can be learned in or out of The Liberal Zone."